The
_Speedy
Question
Bank

Key Stage 3
Tier 4–6

_Speedy Revision

Introduction

This question bank is aimed at Tier 4–6 of the KS3 National Tests for Mathematics. It's the perfect size to keep with you at all times during the crucial weeks before the tests.

There is *speedy* coverage of each topic in the four main strands:
● Number
● Algebra
● Shape, space & measures
● Handling data

Speed-up sheets

The idea behind this book is simple: to provide the *speediest* practice possible. To this end, some questions have a mouse symbol, , next to them. This indicates that a *speed*-up sheet is available for download from our website.

Go to
www.brookworth.co.uk/speedup.html
for links to all the *speed*-up sheets.

The *speed*-up sheets provide blank axes, diagrams to complete and so on. And of course they are all free!

Answers to all questions can be found at the back of the book, so that you can check that you're on the right track.

Good luck in your tests!

Contents

Special numbers

1 Here are the first four square numbers:

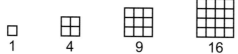

1   4   9   16

Draw the next three square numbers.

2 Here are the first four triangular numbers:

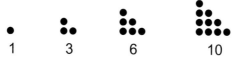

1   3   6   10

Draw the next three triangular numbers.

3 List the first ten prime numbers.

4 10, 43, 17, 25, 23, 64, 36
From the list, write down the
a prime numbers   **b** square numbers   **c** triangular numbers.

Squares & square roots

1 Find these without using a calculator:
a 5^2	**b** 7^2	**c** 10^2
d 4^2	**e** 8^2	**f** 9^2
g 6^2	**h** 70^2	**i** 20^2

2 Use the $\boxed{x^2}$ button on your calculator to find these:
a 3^2	**b** 15^2	**c** 13^2
d 12^2	**e** 50^2	**f** 14^2
g 100^2	**h** 18^2	**i** 21^2

3 Find these without using a calculator:
a $\sqrt{16}$	**b** $\sqrt{49}$	**c** $\sqrt{25}$
d $\sqrt{121}$	**e** $\sqrt{4}$	**f** $\sqrt{64}$

4 Use the $\boxed{\sqrt{}}$ button on your calculator to find these:
a $\sqrt{100}$	**b** $\sqrt{225}$	**c** $\sqrt{196}$
d $\sqrt{400}$	**e** $\sqrt{625}$	**f** $\sqrt{324}$
g $\sqrt{1156}$	**h** $\sqrt{1681}$	**i** $\sqrt{0.09}$

Speedy Revision

Mental strategies for + and –

1 Use near doubles to answer these:

a 40 + 44   b 110 + 120   c 350 + 400
d 79 + 82   e 124 + 126   f 499 + 502
g 309 + 315   h 389 + 396   i 241 + 235

2 Look for pairs totalling 10 to help you with these:

a 1 + 2 + 9 + 8   b 4 + 6 + 6 + 4 + 10
c 4 + 7 + 6 + 2 + 3   d 1 + 2 + 2 + 8 + 9 + 8
e 4 + 25 + 6 + 3 + 7   f 5 + 100 + 7 + 5 + 3

3 Use partitioning to add these:

a 54 + 17   b 129 + 14   c 431 + 56
d 918 + 75   e 238 + 149   f 82 + 709
g 602 + 97   h 116 + 94   i 54 + 762

4 Use partitioning to subtract these:

a 186 – 43   b 599 – 57   c 358 – 107
d 980 – 715   e 649 – 532   f 207 – 84
g 357 – 162   h 411 – 350   i 719 – 682

5 Use compensation to add these:

a 68 + 29   b 211 + 46   c 309 + 78
d 512 + 91   e 775 + 204   f 82 + 99
g 317 + 195   h 446 + 287   i 106 + 649

6 Use compensation to subtract these:

a 95 – 39   b 497 – 68   c 657 – 96
d 480 – 192   e 711 – 508   f 903 – 495
g 317 – 183   h 823 – 475   i 505 – 369

7 For each of these, choose the method you think will be quickest.

a 916 – 49   b 516 + 218   c 753 + 192
d 674 – 236   e 250 + 259   f 402 – 389
g 351 – 219   h 711 + 247   i 142 + 299

8 Add these distances: 213 cm + 154 cm

9 In an electrical shop, a TV costs £268 and a digital camera costs £152. How much more does the TV cost?

Written methods for + and –

1 Use a written method to add these:
- **a** 176 + 122
- **b** 612 + 547
- **c** 845 + 135
- **d** 429 + 315
- **e** 519 + 290
- **f** 1465 + 392

2 Use a written method to subtract these:
- **a** 198 – 174
- **b** 572 – 361
- **c** 265 – 180
- **d** 314 – 152
- **e** 223 – 106
- **f** 1450 – 125

3 Use a written method to add these:
- **a** 1.36 + 1.42
- **b** 21.7 + 18.2
- **c** 5.93 + 2.04
- **d** 4.32 + 1.47
- **e** 2.61 + 1.32
- **f** 117.5 + 43.2

4 Use a written method to subtract these:
- **a** 4.96 – 3.12
- **b** 6.19 – 2.08
- **c** 7.83 – 5.71
- **d** 27.18 – 14.06
- **e** 17.83 – 6.41
- **f** 25.07 – 13.02

5 Use a written method to add these:
- **a** 8.37 + 2.15
- **b** 5.91 + 3.24
- **c** 6.81 + 2.36
- **d** 3.09 + 2.18
- **e** 54.7 + 13.5
- **f** 7.16 + 2.47

6 Use a written method to subtract these:
- **a** 7.94 – 3.75
- **b** 12.71 – 5.09
- **c** 36.9 – 17.46
- **d** 20.4 – 13.21
- **e** 259.08 – 28.16
- **f** 564.12 – 7.8

7 Use a written method to work out these money amounts:
- **a** £18.72 + £21.16
- **b** £27.98 – £16.52
- **c** £25.67 + £14.15
- **d** £48.50 – £7.19

8 Gemma has £37.64 in her purse. She buys a CD for £14.21. How much money does she have left?

9 David is saving up to buy an MP3 player which costs £182.60. He has saved £76.18 so far. How much more does he need to save?

Speedy Revision

Multiplying & dividing by 10, 100, 1000, ...

1 Multiply:
 a 54 × 10   b 9 × 1000   c 5 × 100
 d 6.3 × 10   e 0.8 × 100   f 0.2 × 1000
 g 0.32 × 100   h 0.045 × 1000   i 5.06 × 10

2 Divide:
 a 400 ÷ 100   b 96 ÷ 10   c 20 000 ÷ 1000
 d 319 ÷ 10   e 24.8 ÷ 10   f 71 ÷ 100
 g 111 ÷ 100   h 4160 ÷ 100   i 5100 ÷ 1000

3 Multiply:
 a 9 × 600   b 11 × 70   c 3 × 8000
 d 7 × 3000   e 5 × 400   f 12 × 50

4 Divide:
 a 1600 ÷ 40   b 360 ÷ 900   c 33 000 ÷ 3000
 d 24 ÷ 80   e 48 000 ÷ 600   f 380 ÷ 2000

Mental strategies for × and ÷

1 Double then double again to answer these:
 a 23 × 4   b 16 × 4   c 28 × 4   d 31 × 4

2 Start these by multiplying by 10:
 a 15 × 5   b 39 × 11   c 32 × 20   d 42 × 5
 e 17 × 9   f 23 × 9   g 22 × 11   h 16 × 20

3 Multiply by 100 then use halving to answer these:
 a 30 × 50   b 14 × 50   c 16 × 25   d 32 × 25

4 Multiply by 10, double, then add or subtract the original number to answer these:
 a 15 × 19   b 25 × 19   c 15 × 21   d 12 × 19
 e 25 × 21   f 13 × 21   g 40 × 21   h 30 × 19

5 Use partitioning for these multiplications:
 a 15 × 8   b 14 × 7   c 105 × 6   d 52 × 9
 e 28 × 7   f 102 × 8   g 15 × 11   h 51 × 6

6 Use your times tables to help you answer these:
 a 64 ÷ 8   b 35 ÷ 7   c 132 ÷ 11   d 63 ÷ 9

Written multiplication

1 Use the grid method to answer these:
 a 47 × 9 **b** 8 × 52 **c** 27 × 41 **d** 139 × 6
 e 7 × 205 **f** 13 × 67 **g** 36 × 21 **h** 128 × 12

2 Use the column method to answer these:
 a 39 × 7 **b** 42 × 9 **c** 26 × 17 **d** 34 × 21
 e 28 × 24 **f** 316 × 8 **g** 120 × 19 **h** 241 × 16

3 Use the grid method to answer these:
 a 1.8 × 9 **b** 3.4 × 7 **c** 5.9 × 4 **d** 2.7 × 6
 e 1.24 × 3 **f** 2.76 × 8 **g** 3.19 × 5 **h** 1.65 × 9

4 Use the column method to answer these:
 a 2.6 × 7 **b** 4.1 × 6 **c** 3.7 × 8 **d** 4.9 × 5
 e 3.06 × 9 **f** 1.29 × 8 **g** 2.31 × 7 **h** 4.12 × 6

5 Colleen is planning a picnic.
 A bottle of lemonade costs £2.35.
 Use a written method to find how much
 7 bottles of lemonade will cost.

Written division

1 Use a written method to work out:
 a 126 ÷ 3 **b** 133 ÷ 7 **c** 162 ÷ 6 **d** 153 ÷ 9
 e 245 ÷ 5 **f** 104 ÷ 4 **g** 232 ÷ 8 **h** 176 ÷ 11

2 Write the answers to these with a remainder:
 a 96 ÷ 5 **b** 124 ÷ 9 **c** 128 ÷ 7 **d** 71 ÷ 3
 e 139 ÷ 8 **f** 206 ÷ 5 **g** 124 ÷ 6 **h** 125 ÷ 4

3 Use a written method to work out:
 a 7.2 ÷ 4 **b** 22.5 ÷ 9 **c** 91.7 ÷ 7 **d** 69.6 ÷ 6
 e 61.5 ÷ 3 **f** 175.2 ÷ 8 **g** 244.8 ÷ 12 **h** 151.2 ÷ 9

4 There are 602 strawberries in a basket.
 The strawberries are divided equally between 7 friends.
 Using a written method, find the number of strawberries each
 friend receives.

Multiples, factors & prime factors

1 List the first five multiples of these:

a 2	**b** 4	**c** 10	**d** 7
e 6	**f** 11	**g** 3	**h** 20

2 Write true or false for each of these:

a 2 is a factor of 318.　　**b** 10 is a factor of 50.
c 3 is a factor of 46.　　**d** 2 is a factor of 199.
e 5 is a factor of 1000.　　**f** 4 is a factor of 82.
g 5 is a factor of 51.　　**h** 9 is a factor of 126.

3 List all the factors of these:

a 27	**b** 14	**c** 36	**d** 20
e 100	**f** 63	**g** 49	**h** 44

4 A prime number has exactly two factors.
List the factors of these and state whether they are prime:

a 19	**b** 25	**c** 21	**d** 17

5 3, 18, 25, 27, 32, 12

From the list of numbers, find any
a factors of 36　　**b** multiples of 4.

6 Write these as products of their prime factors:

a 28	**b** 105	**c** 75	**d** 78
e 100	**f** 46	**g** 140	**h** 90

LCM & HCF

1 What is the Least Common Multiple (LCM) of

a 3 and 9	**b** 5 and 8
c 8 and 12	**d** 16 and 24
e 15 and 25	**f** 14 and 21
g 40 and 100	**h** 25 and 30?

2 What is the Highest Common Factor (HCF) of

a 12 and 18	**b** 25 and 35
c 36 and 60	**d** 21 and 49
e 32 and 48	**f** 13 and 63
g 42 and 70	**h** 60 and 105?

Ordering numbers

1 Find the number halfway between 2530 and 2540.

2 Put these numbers in order, smallest first:
   a 181, 99, 152, 27, 15, 17   b 1001, 58, 16, 209, 182
   c 6, 409, 72, 15, 4, 399   d 21, 12, 102, 121, 112
   e 257, 3006, 42, 4, 2, 39   f 96, 102, 531, 480, 482, 79

3 Which is greater:
   a 0.42 or 0.43   b 1.62 or 1.67   c 5.79 or 5.71
   d 1.78 or 1.92   e 30.18 or 30.19   f 0.54 or 0.48
   g 0.3 or 0.05   h 1.8 or 1.29   i 21.05 or 21.3?

4 In the triple jump, Pete jumped 14.19 m and Earl jumped 14.3 m. Who jumped further?

Rounding & estimating

1 Round these to the nearest 10:
   a 32   b 65   c 1071   d 239   e 4015

2 Round these to the nearest 100:
   a 472   b 801   c 49   d 1250   e 1022

3 Round these to the nearest 1000:
   a 2069   b 502   c 7386   d 6915   e 31 200

4 Round these to the nearest whole number:
   a 0.9   b 10.5   c 3.08   d 12.1   e 16.59

5 Round these to 1 d.p.
   a 6.18   b 0.59   c 1.42   d 2.65   e 5.45
   f 3.84   g 4.79   h 7.05   i 1.63   j 3.12

6 Round these to 2 d.p.
   a 1.438   b 9.026   c 4.9415   d 10.835
   e 0.6104 f 2.9945 g 12.095   h 1.7216

7 Do these on a calculator. Check the answers by estimating.
   a 306 + 489   b 897 − 265   c 21 × 38
   d 1209 + 1672   e 35 × 42   f 4117 − 3089
   g 6.9 × 8.7   h 14.6 + 9.2   i 89.1 ÷ 9.9

Negative numbers

1 Write down the temperatures shown on these thermometers:

a 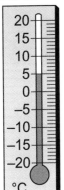   b    c    d

2 Copy this number line:

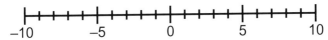

Show these numbers on your number line:
a 3   b −3   c −7   d −9

3 a Write this list of numbers in order of size, smallest first:

−1, 4, −3, 1, 2

b Draw a number line from −5 to 5 and show the numbers in part **a** on it.

4 a The temperature is 5°C. It falls by 10°C. What is the new temperature?

b The temperature is −3°C. It rises by 10°C. What is the new temperature?

c The temperature is −3°C. It falls by 10°C. What is the new temperature?

5 Work out the following:

a 4 − 10   b 10 − 15   c −10 + 20

d −12 + 20   e −12 + 8   f −10 − 20

g −9 − 12   h −40 − 70   i 4 − 5 − 8

j −3 + 8 − 7   k 4 + −1   l −6 − −3

Fractions

1 Write down the fraction that is shaded:

a   b   c

d   e   f

g   h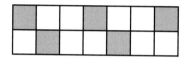

 2 Copy these shapes and shade the given fraction:

a 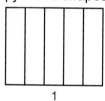 b 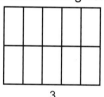 c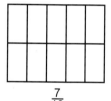

$\frac{1}{5}$ $\frac{3}{10}$ $\frac{7}{10}$

3 Write two equivalent fractions for the shaded part:

a   b   c

d   e   f

Speedy Revision

continued

Fractions (continued)

4 Copy these and finish simplifying the fractions:

a
$$\frac{3}{6} = \frac{\square}{2}$$
(÷3, ÷3)

b
$$\frac{4}{6} = \frac{\square}{3}$$
(÷2, ÷2)

c
$$\frac{6}{9} = \frac{2}{\square}$$
(÷3, ÷3)

d
$$\frac{4}{8} = \frac{1}{\square}$$
(÷4, ÷4)

e
$$\frac{8}{20} = \frac{\square}{\square}$$
(÷4, ÷4)

f
$$\frac{2}{14} = \frac{\square}{\square}$$
(÷2, ÷2)

g
$$\frac{6}{15} = \frac{2}{5}$$
(÷□, ÷□)

h
$$\frac{5}{20} = \frac{1}{4}$$
(÷□, ÷□)

i
$$\frac{8}{12} = \frac{\square}{3}$$
(÷□, ÷□)

5 Write as a fraction in its simplest form:

a $\frac{6}{8}$

b $\frac{2}{12}$

c $\frac{10}{30}$

d $\frac{3}{18}$

e $\frac{9}{27}$

f $\frac{6}{24}$

g 6p out of 10p

h 5p out of 50p

i 25p out of £1

6 Make sure the fractions have the same denominator before you add them:

a $\frac{1}{5} + \frac{1}{5}$

b $\frac{1}{8} + \frac{1}{8} + \frac{1}{8}$

c $\frac{1}{9} + \frac{1}{9} + \frac{1}{9} + \frac{1}{9}$

d $\frac{2}{7} + \frac{1}{7}$

e $\frac{4}{6} + \frac{1}{6}$

f $\frac{3}{8} + \frac{1}{8} + \frac{1}{8}$

g $\frac{3}{7} + \frac{2}{7} + \frac{1}{7}$

h $\frac{1}{4} + \frac{1}{8}$

i $\frac{2}{3} + \frac{1}{6}$

7 Make sure the fractions have the same denominator before you do the calculation:

a $\frac{2}{3} - \frac{1}{3}$

b $\frac{2}{5} - \frac{1}{5}$

c $\frac{4}{7} - \frac{3}{7}$

d $\frac{1}{5} + \frac{1}{5} + \frac{1}{5} - \frac{1}{5}$

e $\frac{5}{8} - \frac{2}{8}$

f $\frac{4}{8} + \frac{3}{8} - \frac{2}{8}$

g $\frac{8}{9} - \frac{5}{9} - \frac{1}{9}$

h $\frac{2}{3} - \frac{5}{9}$

i $\frac{4}{6} - \frac{1}{2}$

8 Simplify the answers to these:

a $\frac{2}{6} + \frac{1}{6}$

b $\frac{1}{9} + \frac{1}{9} + \frac{1}{9}$

c $\frac{3}{10} + \frac{1}{10} + \frac{1}{10}$

d $\frac{5}{8} + \frac{2}{8} - \frac{1}{8}$

e $\frac{11}{12} - \frac{8}{12}$

f $\frac{6}{10} - \frac{2}{10} - \frac{2}{10}$

g $\frac{7}{16} + \frac{3}{16} + \frac{2}{16}$

h $\frac{2}{5} + \frac{1}{10}$

i $\frac{6}{12} - \frac{1}{3}$

continued ➤➤

Speedy Revision

Fractions (continued)

9 Write these mixed numbers as improper fractions:

a $1\frac{1}{2}$ b $1\frac{1}{3}$ c $1\frac{3}{4}$

d $1\frac{2}{5}$ e $2\frac{1}{6}$ f $2\frac{3}{7}$

g $2\frac{5}{8}$ h $3\frac{1}{10}$ i $3\frac{2}{9}$

10 Write these improper fractions as mixed numbers:

a $\frac{11}{3}$ b $\frac{13}{2}$ c $\frac{25}{6}$

d $\frac{17}{5}$ e $\frac{20}{9}$ f $\frac{21}{4}$

g $\frac{10}{4}$ h $\frac{19}{8}$ i $\frac{22}{7}$

11 Put these in order, smallest first:

a $\frac{1}{2}$ $\frac{9}{12}$ $\frac{2}{3}$

b $\frac{11}{18}$ $\frac{4}{9}$ $\frac{2}{3}$

c $\frac{3}{4}$ $\frac{13}{20}$ $\frac{3}{5}$

12 Which is bigger:

a $5\frac{1}{2}$ or $\frac{9}{2}$?   b $1\frac{1}{4}$ or $\frac{7}{4}$?

13 Find: a $\frac{1}{3}$ of £90   b $\frac{2}{3}$ of £90

14 Find: a $\frac{1}{4}$ of 100 m   b $\frac{3}{4}$ of 100 m

15 Find: a $\frac{1}{5}$ of 35 mm   b $\frac{2}{5}$ of 35 mm

16 Find: a $\frac{1}{10}$ of 40p   b $\frac{7}{10}$ of 40p

17 What is $\frac{2}{3}$ of 360°?

18 What is $\frac{3}{5}$ of 50 g?

19 Give the answers to these multiplications in simplest form:

a $\frac{1}{2} \times \frac{1}{3}$ b $\frac{1}{3} \times \frac{2}{5}$ c $\frac{2}{3} \times \frac{3}{7}$

20 Do these divisions:

a $\frac{1}{3} \div \frac{1}{2}$ b $\frac{1}{2} \div \frac{5}{7}$ c $\frac{1}{5} \div \frac{3}{4}$

Speedy Revision

Percentages

1   In a class of 30 students, 12 are girls.
    What percentage of the class are girls?

2   In a pack of 52 playing cards, 13 are Spades.
    What percentage of the pack are Spades?

3   A sofa is priced at £2500.
    In a sale, the price of the sofa is reduced by £750.
    What is this reduction as a percentage?

4   Do these by finding 10% first:
    a 5% of £30   b 40% of 90 g

5   Do these by finding 1% first:
    a 17% of 80 cm   b 36% of 150p

6   Find:
    a 25% of 800 ml   b 30% of £40
    c 4% of 150 g   d 72% of 25 mm
    e 21% of £450   f 59% of 30 m

7   Increase:
    a 30p by 10%   b 15 mm by 20%
    c 120 g by 5%   d 80 m by 25%
    e £48 by 30%   f 50 litres by 17%

8   Decrease:
    a 70p by 10%   b 60 mm by 5%
    c £24 by 20%   d 140 g by 15%
    e £20 000 by 8%   f 50 litres by 32%

9   In a sale, all prices are reduced by 20%.
    What is the sale price of a T-shirt that originally cost £12?

10 A plant was 84 mm tall in April.
    By May, the plant was 25% taller.
    How tall was the plant in May?

11 A bank account pays 5% interest.
    There is £230 in the account before interest is added.
    How much is in the account after interest is added?

Fractions, decimals & percentages

1 Convert these fractions to decimals:

   a $\frac{1}{100}$ **b** $\frac{1}{8}$ **c** $\frac{3}{5}$ **d** $\frac{7}{8}$

   e $\frac{3}{20}$ **f** $\frac{27}{50}$ **g** $\frac{1}{3}$ **h** $\frac{3}{10}$

2 Convert these percentages to fractions in their simplest form:

   a 17%   **b** 23%   **c** 3%   **d** 29%

   e 30%   **f** 75%   **g** 15%   **h** 12%

3 Convert these fractions to percentages:

   a $\frac{5}{100}$ **b** $\frac{62}{100}$ **c** $\frac{18}{100}$ **d** $\frac{94}{100}$

   e $\frac{3}{10}$ **f** $\frac{1}{10}$ **g** $\frac{1}{3}$ **h** $\frac{4}{5}$

4 Convert these percentages to decimals:

   a 40%   **b** 25%   **c** 90%   **d** 60%

   e 50%   **f** 18%   **g** 32%   **h** 99%

5 Convert these decimals to fractions:

   a 0.5   **b** 0.1   **c** 0.75   **d** 0.7

   e 0.6   **f** 0.13   **g** 0.49   **h** 0.45

6 Which is the bigger amount: 25% of £60 or $\frac{2}{5}$ of £40?

Ratio & proportion

1 What proportion of the squares in each pattern are grey?
Give your answer as a fraction in its simplest form.

   a

   b

   c

   d

   e

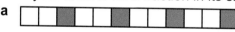
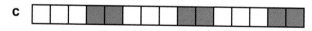

2 Look again at the diagrams in question **1**.
What proportion of the squares in each pattern are white?
Give your answer as a fraction in its simplest form.

Speedy Revision

continued ⟶»

Ratio & proportion (continued)

3 Look again at the diagrams in question **1**.
What is the ratio of grey squares to white squares?
Give each answer in its simplest form.

4 In a class there are 16 boys and 14 girls.
Write the ratio of boys to girls in its simplest form.

5 On a bus, there are 20 people. 12 are female.
Write the ratio of females to males in its simplest form.

6 1 kg of red onions costs 35p.
How much would 3 kg of red onions cost?

7 1 kg of apples costs £1.20.
How much would 5 kg cost?

8 7 apples cost £1.75.
How much would 3 apples cost?

9 5 chocolate bars cost £1.60.
How much would 9 chocolate bars cost?

10 A recipe for 4 people uses 160 g of soya mince.
How much soya mince is needed for 7 people?

Calculations with brackets

1 Work these out on paper then check your answers on a
calculator:
a $18 \div 2 + 4$
b $18 + 4 \div 2$
c $18 \div (2 + 4)$
d $5 \times 2 + 6$
e $5 \times (2 + 6)$
f $5 \times 6 + 2$
g $16 - 3 + 9$
h $(16 - 3) + 9$
i $16 - (3 + 9)$
j $3 \times (4 + 2) - 7$

2 Insert brackets if they are needed:
a $21 + 7 - 4 = 24$
b $15 - 3 + 2 = 10$
c $8 \times 4 + 6 = 80$
d $3 + 8 \times 12 = 132$
e $36 \div 6 + 3 = 4$
f $4 \times 5 - 18 \div 3 = 14$
g $7 \times 8 - 3 \div 5 = 7$
h $20 - 10 \div 2 = 15$
i $8 + 7 - 3 \times 4 = 48$
j $5 \times 8 \div 4 = 10$

Using letters

1 I have *b* bangles.
I buy a new bangle.
How many bangles do I have now?

2 Sara has *c* chips on her plate.
Kate has 3 more.
How many chips does Kate have?

3 There are *s* sweets in a bag.
Luka eats one sweet.
How many sweets are left?

4 There are *m* marbles on the table.
2 marbles fall onto the floor.
How many marbles are left on the table?

5 There are *c* counters in a jar.
How many counters are there in 10 jars?

6 There are *b* bristles on one brush.
How many bristles are there on 5 brushes?

7 Write these in 'shorthand':
  a $2 \times g$ 　　　　**b** $5 \times c$ 　　　　**c** $3 \times t$
  d $n \times m$ 　　　　**e** $y \times z$ 　　　　**f** $a \times b$
  g $10 \times r \times s$ 　　**h** $4 \times p \times q$ 　**i** $7 \times c \times d$

8 Simplify these expressions by collecting like terms:
  a $y + y + y$ 　　　　　　**b** $z + z + z + z$
  c $a + 3a$ 　　　　　　　　**d** $p + p + 5p$
  e $d + d + d - d$ 　　　　　**f** $8s - 2s$
  g $n + 4n - 2n$ 　　　　　　**h** $2r + 3r + 6r + 5r$
  i $3b + 3b + 3b + 3b + 3b$ 　**j** $16t - 4t - 3t + t$

9 Simplify these expressions by collecting like terms:
  a $w + w + 6$ 　　　　　　**b** $2y + 3 + y$
  c $10s + 1 - 2s + 5$ 　　　　**d** $8 + a + 4a - 2$
  e $2n + 1 + 2n + 1$ 　　　　**f** $m + 5m + m + 3 - 1$
  g $7 + b + 8b - 2b - 5$ 　　　**h** $3c + 3 + c + 3c$
  i $6t + 2t + 3 - t + 4 + t$ 　　**j** $g + g + 8 + 3g - g$

Speedy Revision

Brackets & algebraic fractions

1 Multiply out these brackets:

  a $2(x + 1)$ **b** $5(y - 3)$ **c** $3(n + 2)$

  d $8(a - b)$ **e** $-4(c + 1)$ **f** $6(x + 5)$

  g $-3(z + 4)$ **h** $10(w - 1)$ **i** $-2(t - 1)$

2 Simplify these expressions:

  a $3(a + 1) + 2$ **b** $2(n - 3) + n$

  c $5(4 - p) - 8$ **d** $10 - 2(z + 1)$

3 Add these fractions:

  a $\frac{x}{5} + \frac{x}{5}$ **b** $\frac{x}{3} + \frac{x}{3}$ **c** $\frac{2x}{8} + \frac{x}{8}$

  d $\frac{z}{7} + \frac{z}{7} + \frac{z}{7}$ **e** $\frac{4d}{10} + \frac{3d}{10}$ **f** $\frac{5n}{2} + \frac{4n}{2}$

  g $\frac{8a}{3} - \frac{a}{3}$ **h** $\frac{3a}{4} + \frac{2a}{4}$ **i** $\frac{4m}{9} - \frac{3m}{9}$

Equations

1 Solve these equations:

  a $x + 8 = 10$ **b** $5x = 50$

  c $3p = 9$ **d** $m + 5 = 9$

  e $p - 2 = 31$ **f** $2x = 18$

  g $3y = 27$ **h** $c - 4 = 3$

  i $4y = 16$ **j** $a + 14 = 30$

2 Solve these equations:

  a $2x + 1 = 5$ **b** $5x - 1 = 19$

  c $3x - 3 = 9$ **d** $4x + 5 = 25$

  e $2x + 8 = 28$ **f** $7x - 2 = 12$

  g $3x + 7 = 34$ **h** $8x - 4 = 36$

  i $5x - 7 = 33$ **j** $9x + 2 = 29$

3 Solve these equations:

  a $2x = x + 3$ **b** $3x = 2x + 7$

  c $5x = 4x + 11$ **d** $6x = x + 10$

  e $13x = x + 48$ **f** $4x = x + 15$

  g $7x = 4x + 12$ **h** $12x = 7x + 25$

  i $9x = 2x + 14$ **j** $10x = 3x + 42$

continued →

Equations (continued)

4 Solve these equations:

a $2(x + 1) = 6$ **b** $5(x - 2) = 35$
c $3(x + 5) = 27$ **d** $6(x + 4) = 42$
e $4(x - 8) = 12$ **f** $7(x - 3) = 14$
g $3(2x + 1) = 3$ **h** $10(9x + 1) = 100$
i $2(3x - 9) = 6$ **j** $4(2x + 1) = 20$

5 Here is a regular hexagon:

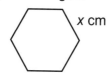

x cm

The length of each side of the hexagon is x centimetres.

a Write an expression for the perimeter of the hexagon in terms of x.

b Find the value of x if the perimeter of the hexagon is 42 cm.

Formulae & substitution

1 Substitute $m = 8$ into each of these expressions:

a $m + 3$ **b** $m - 5$ **c** $m + 6$
d $3m$ **e** $10m$ **f** $7m$
g $2m + 4$ **h** $3m - 5$ **i** $5m + 9$

2 Use the formula

> Number of millimetres = 10 × number of centimetres

to convert these lengths to millimetres:

a 5 cm **b** 13 cm **c** 7 cm
d 8 cm **e** 25 cm **f** 11 cm

3 Use the formula

> $c = 100m$ where c = number of centimetres,
> m = number of metres

to convert these lengths to centimetres:

a 2 metres **b** 5 metres **c** 1.5 metres
d 10 metres **e** 0.8 metre **f** 2.4 metres

Speedy Revision

continued ⟶»

Formulae & substitution (continued)

4 A joiner charges £22 per hour.
   a Write a formula for the charge, C, in terms of the number of hours worked, h.
   b Use your formula to work out the charge for 5 hours.
   c Use your formula to work out the charge for 7 hours.

5 This is the formula for finding speed:

   Speed = Distance ÷ Time
   a A car travels 180 miles in 3 hours.
      What is the speed of the car?
   b Re-write this formula using the letters S = Speed, D = Distance, T = Time.
   c Find S if D = 100 miles, T = 4 hours.
   d Find S if D = 89 metres, T = 10 seconds.

6 Substitute $p = 2$, $q = 3$, $r = 5$ into these expressions:
   a p^2 **b** $2q^2$ **c** $2 + r^2$
   d $10(p + q)$ **e** $r^2 - p$ **f** $8pq$

7 This is the formula for finding the volume of a cube:

   $V = w^3$
   Find the volume of a cube with w = 5 cm.

Sequences & number patterns

1 This sequence starts at 3 and the rule is 'add 1':
   3, 4, 5, 6, 7, ...
   Write the first five terms of these sequences:
   a Start at 1 and add 2   **b** Start at 5 and add 3
   c Start at 8 and add 1   **d** Start at 20 and subtract 2
   e Start at 2 and double   **f** Start at 30 and subtract 5
   g Start at 144 and halve   **h** Start at 4 and multiply by 3

2 Write the start number and rule for these sequences:
   a 2, 4, 6, 8, 10, ...   **b** 5, 10, 15, 20, 25, ...
   c 100, 99, 98, 97, 96, ...   **d** 4, 10, 16, 22, 28, ...
   e 36, 30, 24, 18, 12, ...   **f** 1, 3, 9, 27, 81, ...
   g 800, 400, 200, 100, 50, ... **h** 5, 10, 20, 40, 80, ...

continued ⟶»

Sequences & number patterns (cont)

3 Write the next three terms for these sequences:
- **a** 3, 6, 9, 12, ...
- **b** 10, 20, 30, 40, ...
- **c** 1, 2, 4, 8, 16, ...
- **d** 90, 85, 80, 75, ...
- **e** 7, 12, 17, 22, ...
- **f** 20, 18, 16, 14, ...
- **g** 320, 160, 80, 40, ...
- **h** 14, 17, 20, 23, ...

4 Here is a sequence of diagrams:

- **a** Draw the next two diagrams in the sequence.
- **b** Describe in words how the sequence grows.
- **c** How many squares will the 8th and 10th diagrams need?
- **d** Write an expression for the nth term of the pattern.

5 Here is a sequence of matchstick patterns:

- **a** Draw the next two diagrams in the sequence.
- **b** Describe in words how the sequence grows.
- **c** How many matchsticks will the 8th and 10th diagrams need?
- **d** Write an expression for the nth term of the pattern.

6 Write the first five terms of the sequence with nth term:
- **a** $n + 5$
- **b** $6n$
- **c** $n - 1$
- **d** $10n$
- **e** $2n + 1$
- **f** $5n - 1$
- **g** $3n + 4$
- **h** $20 - n$
- **i** $5n - 2$

7 The nth term of a sequence is $100 - 2n$.
Find these terms in the sequence:
- **a** 1st term
- **b** 15th term
- **c** 30th term

8 Work out the nth term in these sequences:
- **a** 2, 4, 6, 8, 10, ...
- **b** 5, 10, 15, 20, 25, ...
- **c** 8, 9, 10, 11, 12, ...
- **d** 101, 102, 103, 104, 105, ...
- **e** 3, 5, 7, 9, 11, ...
- **f** 1, 3, 5, 7, 9, ...

Functions & mappings

1 **a** Find the outputs for this function machine:

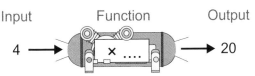

Input	Function	Output
3		?
5	– 4	?
10		?
x		?

b If the output is zero, what is the input?

2 Complete the function for this function machine:

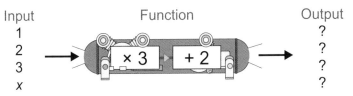

Input   Function   Output

4 → × .... → 20

3 **a** Find the outputs for this function machine:

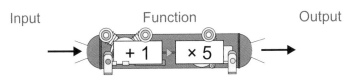

Input	Function	Output
1		?
2	× 3 + 2	?
3		?
x		?

b Find the input when the output is 17.

4 Draw a mapping diagram for this function machine:

Input   Function   Output

→ + 1 × 5 →

Use 1, 2, 3 as the inputs.

5 Write the function for the machine in question **4** using algebra: $x \rightarrow ...$

6 Draw mapping diagrams with inputs 1, 2, 3 for these functions:

a $x \rightarrow 4x$ **b** $x \rightarrow 2x - 5$ **c** $x \rightarrow 3(x + 1)$

Coordinates

1 **a** Write down the coordinates of points A and D.

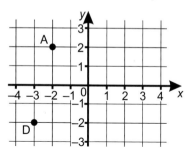

b Copy the diagram and plot the points B(1, 2) and C(2, −2).

c Join the four points. What shape have you drawn?

2 Write down the coordinates of the points A to J.

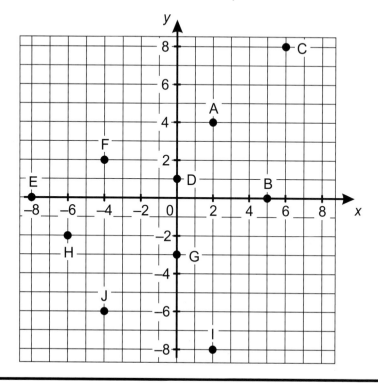

Speedy Revision

Straight-line graphs

1 **a** Copy and complete this table of values for the equation
$y = x + 2$:

x	−3	−2	−1	0	1
$y = x + 2$				2	

b Copy this grid and draw the graph of $y = x + 2$.

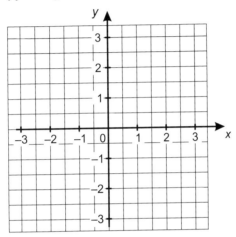

2 Find the gradient of each of these lines:

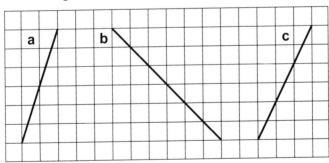

3 State whether the equation is for a horizontal, vertical or
diagonal graph:

a $y = 2x$ **b** $y = 10$ **c** $y = 3x$
d $x = -2$ **e** $y = x + 1$ **f** $y = x - 1$
g $y = 0$ **h** $y = 4x - 3$ **i** $x = 5$

continued

Straight-line graphs (continued)

4 **a** Copy and complete this table of values for the equation
$y = 2x + 3$:

x	−3	−2	−1	0	1	2
$y = 2x + 3$	−3			3		

b Copy this grid and draw the graph of $y = 2x + 3$:

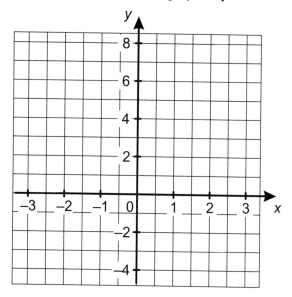

5 Match these equations to their graphs:

$$y = x, \ y = 4, \ x = 4, \ y = -x$$

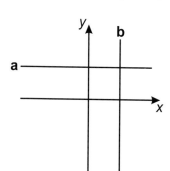

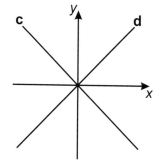

Real-life graphs

1 **a** £1 is roughly €1.40.
Use this fact to copy and complete the table.

Amount in pounds	0	10	20	30	40	50
Amount in euros	0	14				

b Plot the points
from your table
on a grid like this:

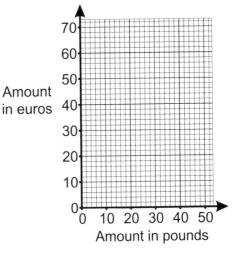

Amount in euros

Amount in pounds

2 The graph shows Jenny's cycle to and from a local shop.
On her way home, she meets her sister, Susie.
At this point Jenny gets off her bike and walks with Susie.
Use the letters to explain what each part of the graph shows.

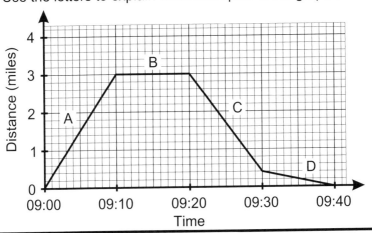

Distance (miles)

Time

Units of measurement

1 How many:
- **a** centimetres in a metre
- **b** millimetres in a centimetre
- **c** metres in a kilometre
- **d** grams in a kilogram
- **e** millilitres in a litre?

2 How many:
- **a** inches in a foot
- **b** feet in a yard
- **c** ounces in a pound
- **d** pints in a gallon?

3 Roughly how many:
- **a** centimetres in a foot
- **b** kilometres in a mile
- **c** grams in a pound
- **d** grams in an ounce
- **e** pints in a litre?

4 Convert each of these measurements into centimetres:
- **a** 3 m
- **b** 4 m
- **c** 10 m
- **d** 23 m
- **e** 50 m
- **f** 0.5 m

5 Convert each of these measurements into millimetres:
- **a** 2 cm
- **b** 5 cm
- **c** 11 cm
- **d** 36 cm
- **e** 75 cm
- **f** 1.5 cm

6 Convert each of these measurements into metres:
- **a** 3 km
- **b** 4 km
- **c** 10 km
- **d** 23 km
- **e** 50 km
- **f** 2.5 km

7 Convert each of these measurements:
- **a** 2 kg to grams
- **b** 5 kg to grams
- **c** 15 kg to grams
- **d** 3 litres to millilitres
- **e** 9 litres to millilitres
- **f** 18 litres to millilitres

8 Convert each of these measurements:
- **a** 200 mm to centimetres
- **b** 3000 m to kilometres
- **c** 800 cm to metres
- **d** 5000 ml to litres
- **e** 7000 g to kilograms
- **f** 14 000 ml to litres

9 Convert each of these measurements:
- **a** 45 mm to centimetres
- **b** 500 g to kilograms
- **c** 6500 ml to litres
- **d** 6.2 cm to millimetres
- **e** 1.5 m to centimetres
- **f** 0.5 km to metres

Tier 4–6

Appropriate units & reading scales

1 Which metric units would you use to measure these?
  a height of a desk lamp   **b** width of a house
  c liquid on a teaspoon   **d** mass of a car wheel
  e water in a fish tank   **f** mass of a pencil
  g diameter of a marble   **h** distance from York to Leeds

2 Measure the lengths of these lines to the nearest millimetre:
  a   **b**

  c

3 Write down the value shown on each of these scales:

a 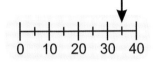   **b**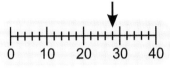

c 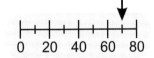   **d**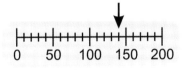

e    **f**

Estimating & measuring angles

1 How many degrees are there in:
   a a quarter turn   **b** a half turn
   c a three-quarter turn   **d** a full turn?

2 For each of these angles:
   i first estimate its size
   ii then measure the angle.

a 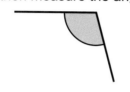   **b**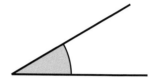

c 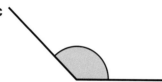   **d**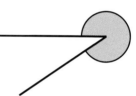

Angles & parallel lines

1 Which of these angles are acute, obtuse, reflex or right angles?

a    **b**

c 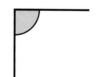   **d**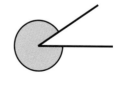

2 **a** What do the angles on a straight line add up to?
    b What do the angles around a point add up to?
    c What sort of angles are formed when two straight lines cross?

Speedy Revision

continued ⟩⟩⟩

Angles & parallel lines (continued)

3 Find the size of the unknown angles:

a
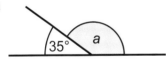

b
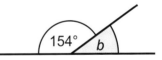

c
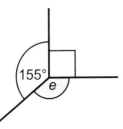

d
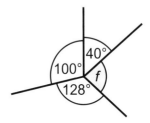

e
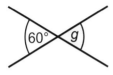

f
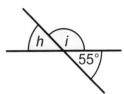

4 On a copy of the diagram, show:
  a the alternate angle to angle P (label it A)
  b the corresponding angle to angle P (label it C).

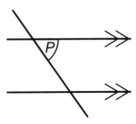

5 Find the size of the unknown angles:

a
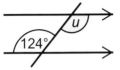

b

c
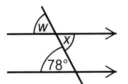

d
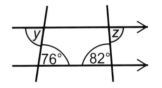

Polygons

1 **a** What do the angles in a triangle add up to?

   b What do the angles in a quadrilateral add up to?

2 Find the size of the unknown angles:

a
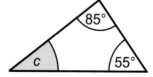

b
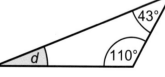

c
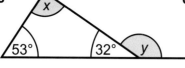

d
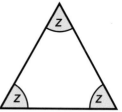

3 Find the size of the unknown angles:

a

b
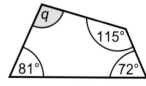

c
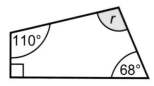

d
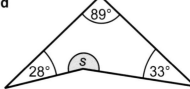

4 Complete these formulae for angles in a polygon:

   a Sum of exterior angles = ...°

   b Sum of interior angles = (number of sides − ......) × ....°

5 **a** How many interior angles does a hexagon have?

   b Calculate the size of an interior angle of a regular hexagon.

   c What is the size of an exterior angle of a regular hexagon?

Symmetry & properties of shapes

1 Copy each shape and then draw its lines of symmetry.

a

b

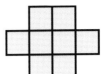

c

d

2 For each of these shapes:
   i write down the number of lines of symmetry
   ii state the order of rotation symmetry.

a

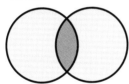

b

c

d

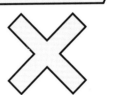

3 Which of these letters have:
   a reflection symmetry
   b rotation symmetry
   c no symmetry?

A E F H
M N P S
T U W Z

4 How many planes of symmetry do these shapes have?

a

b

Equilateral triangular prism

Square-based pyramid

continued ➤➤➤

Speedy Revision

33

Symmetry & properties of shapes (cont)

5 Name these polygons:

a   b 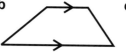 c

d  e   f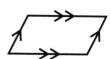

6 Copy and complete this table.

Name of polygon	Number of sides	All sides equal?	All angles equal?	Number of lines of symmetry	Order of rotation symmetry
Square					
Rectangle					
Isosceles triangle					
Equilateral triangle					
Rhombus					
Kite					
Trapezium					
Regular pentagon					
	4	No	No	0	2

Reflection

1 Reflect these shapes in the mirror lines:

a
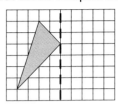

b
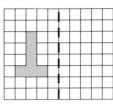

c
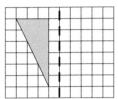

d
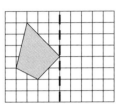

2 Reflect these shapes in the mirror lines:

a
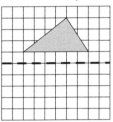

b
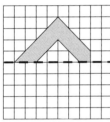

c
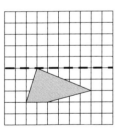

d
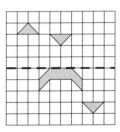

3 Reflect the shape in both mirror lines to make a symmetrical pattern:

Rotation

1 Rotate these shapes 90° clockwise about the dots:

a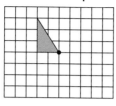

b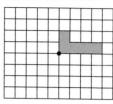

c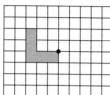

d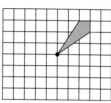

2 Rotate these shapes 90° anticlockwise about the dots:

a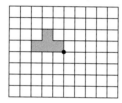

b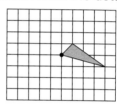

c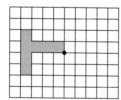

d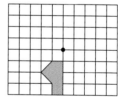

3 Rotate these shapes 180° about the dots:

a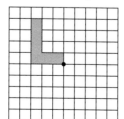

b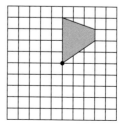

Translation

1 Translate these shapes 3 squares to the right and 2 down.

a 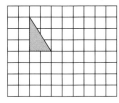　　　　**b**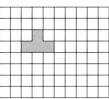

2 Translate these shapes 4 squares to the left and 3 down.

a 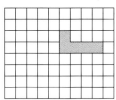　　　　**b**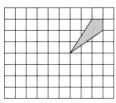

3 Translate these shapes 5 squares to the left and 4 up.

a 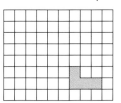　　　　**b**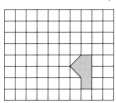

4 Describe these translations:

  a A to B
  b B to C
  c C to D
  d D to E
  e E to F
  f F to G
  g G to H
  h H to I

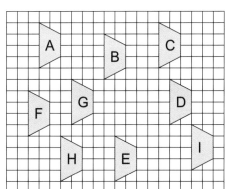

Enlargement

 1 Copy these shapes on squared paper.
Enlarge each shape by scale factor 2.

a   **b**   **c**

 2 Copy these shapes on squared paper.
Enlarge each shape by scale factor 3.

a   **b**   **c**

3 Find the scale factor of these enlargements:

a 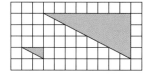   **b**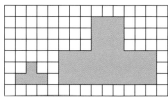

 4 Copy this diagram.
Enlarge the shape using
scale factor 2 and
centre (0, 0).

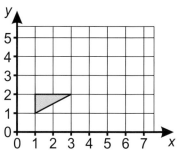

5 **a** Find the scale factor
of this enlargement.
b Find the coordinates
of the centre of
enlargement.

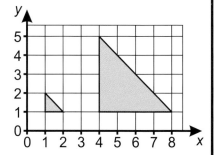

Perimeter & circumference

1 Find the perimeter of each of these shapes.

a

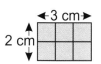

b

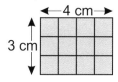

c

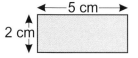

d

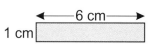

2 Find the perimeter of each of these shapes:

a

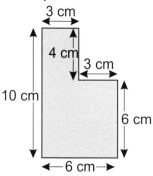

b

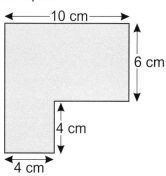

3 Find the circumference of each of these circles:

a

b

c

4 Find the perimeter of these shapes:

a

b

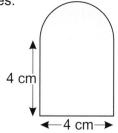

Area of 2-D shapes

1 Find the area of each of these shapes.
Remember to state the units of your answer.

a

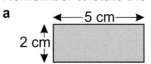

b

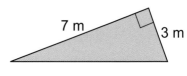

c

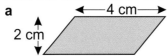

d

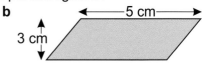

2 Find the area of each shape in question **2** on the previous page (page 39).

3 Find the area of each of these parallelograms:

a

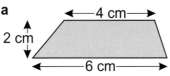

b

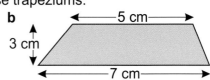

4 Find the area of each of these trapeziums:

a

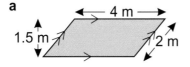

b

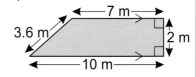

5 Find the area of each of these shapes:

a

b

6 Find the area of each of these circles:

a

b

c

Nets & 3-D shapes; plans & elevations

1 Which of these nets will fold to make a cube?

a   **b**   **c**

2 Name the 3-D shapes that these nets make:

a   **b**   **c**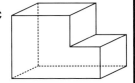

3 Sketch a net for each of these shapes:

a 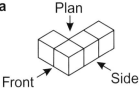   **b**   **c**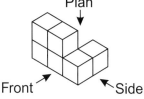

4 For each of these shapes, draw a front elevation, a side elevation and a plan view.

a 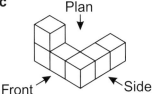   **b**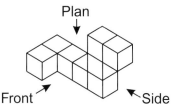

c 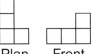   **d**

5 Here are the three views of two solid shapes.
Draw each shape on isometric paper.

a

Plan	Front	Side

b

Plan	Front	Side

Surface area

1 These shapes are made with centimetre cubes.
Find the surface area of each shape.

a

b

c

d
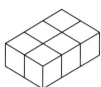

e

f

2 Find the surface area of these shapes:

a
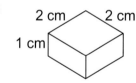
2 cm   2 cm
1 cm

b
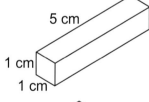
5 cm
1 cm
1 cm

c
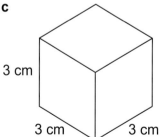
3 cm
3 cm   3 cm

d
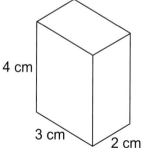
4 cm
3 cm   2 cm

3 The surface area of a cube is 96 m².
Find the length of a side of the cube.

Volume

1   These shapes are made with centimetre cubes.
Find the volume of each shape.

a
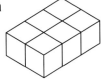

b

c
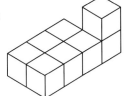

2   Find the volume of these shapes:

a

2 cm   2 cm
1 cm

b
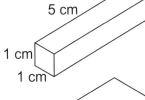
5 cm
1 cm
1 cm

c
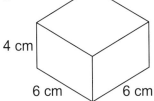
4 cm
6 cm   6 cm

d
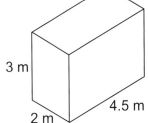
3 m
2 m   4.5 m

3   For each triangular prism find:
i   the area of the triangular end
ii the volume of the prism.

a
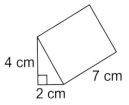
4 cm
2 cm   7 cm

b
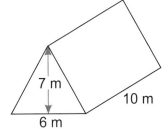
7 m
6 m   10 m

4   The area of the cross-section
of this prism is 24 m².
Find the volume of the prism.
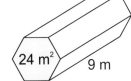
24 m²   9 m

Bearings & scale drawings

1 Use a protractor to find the bearing of B from A in each of these diagrams:

a

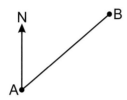

b

2 A map has a scale of 1 cm = 50 km.
How far in real life are these lengths on the map?
a 3 cm   **b** 5 cm   **c** 20 cm

3 A diagram is drawn using a scale of 1 cm represents 20 cm.
How long on the diagram would these real-life lengths be?
a 40 cm   **b** 200 cm   **c** 10 cm

4 The following diagram is drawn using a scale of 1 cm to represent 2 km.

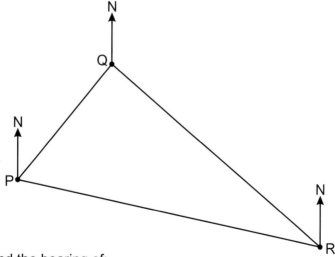

Find the bearing of:
a R from Q   **b** Q from P   **c** P from Q.

Find the distance from:
d P to Q   **e** P to R   **f** Q to R.

Constructions & loci

1 Copy the diagram and construct the perpendicular bisector of the line AB. Clearly show your construction marks.

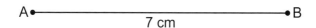

A•————————————————————•B
7 cm

2 Using a ruler and compasses construct an equilateral triangle with sides of 5 cm.

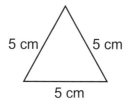

5 cm   5 cm

5 cm

3 The road between Milton and Newham is 8 km long and completely straight.

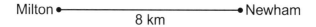

Milton •————————————————• Newham
8 km

a Draw a scale diagram of the road using a scale of 1 cm to 1 km.

b Using compasses find the midpoint of the road between Milton and Newham. Clearly show your construction marks.

4 Dave stands on a line.
He kicks a football on a
path perpendicular to the line.

Copy the diagram below and construct a line to show the path of the ball.

————————•————————
Ball

continued ⟶≫

Constructions & loci (continued)

5   A goat is tethered to a post with a 10 m piece of rope.

Draw a plan diagram to show the region that the goat can reach. Use a scale of 1 cm to 2 m.

6   In a garden, the South wall is perpendicular to the East wall.

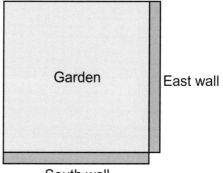

Garden   East wall

South wall

There is a path in the garden such that anyone who walks along it is always the same distance from the South wall as the East wall.
Draw a diagram to show the position of the path.

7   *Hurry Curry* will deliver takeaways within a 4 mile radius.
Tandoori Express will deliver within a 3 mile radius.
The takeaway restaurants are 5 miles apart.

Hurry Curry ●◄————————►● Tandoori Express
                    5 miles

Draw a diagram, using a scale of 2 cm to 1 mile, to show the region that both takeaway restaurants deliver to.

Collecting data & two-way tables

1 Jenny would like to know people's opinions about her local swimming pool. She designs the following questionnaire:

Question 1	How often do you go swimming? Never ☐, occasionally ☐, frequently ☐
Question 2	Do you agree that the swimming pool is good value for money? Yes ☐, no ☐
Question 3	How much do you earn per year? £9999 or less ☐, £10 000 to £19 999 ☐, £20 000 to £29 999 ☐, £30 000 or more ☐

Jenny's teacher says that all of her questions need changing.
a State a fault for each question.

Jenny intends to conduct her survey outside the swimming pool on a Monday morning.
b Give two reasons why this is unsuitable.

2 Explain the difference between primary and secondary data.

3 Copy and complete the two-way table that shows the number of MP3 and MP4 players owned by a group of friends.

	MP3	MP4	Total
Boys own	15		
Girls own		3	
Total	32		41

4 The two-way table shows the colours and brands (Trek or Giant) of some racing bikes in a cycle shop.
Copy and complete the table to find the total number of bikes.

	Red	Blue	Silver	Total
Trek	3			9
Giant		6	4	
Total	8		6	

Frequency tables

 1 Sandy has noted down the colours of 20 revision books. Here is her data:

yellow, orange, purple, purple, purple, orange, orange, yellow, purple, orange, purple, yellow, purple, purple, yellow, purple, orange, purple, yellow, purple

Copy and complete this frequency table for the data.

Colour of book	Tally	Frequency
Yellow		
Orange		
Purple		
Total		

 2 Daphne counted the number of people in 15 cars passing her house. Here is her data:

3, 1, 2, 1, 3, 2, 4, 1, 4, 2, 1, 2, 5, 2, 3

Draw a frequency table to show her data.

 3 Liam counted the number of potatoes in 20 bags. Here are his results:

29, 35, 42, 46, 34, 48, 28, 33, 43, 39,
27, 30, 44, 52, 45, 51, 39, 40, 38, 51

a Copy and complete this frequency table for the data.

Number of potatoes	Tally	Frequency
26 to 35		
36 to 45		
46 to 55		
Total		

b Re-draw the frequency table using the intervals:
$20 \leq N < 30$, $30 \leq N < 40$, $40 \leq N < 50$, $50 \leq N < 60$, where N is the number of potatoes.

Bar charts & line graphs

1 The bar chart shows the number of medals that Middlehampton School won in a swimming competition.

How many medals did the school win in total?

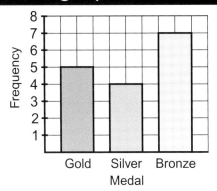

2 Draw a bar chart to represent the data in the table below.

Make of car	Honda	Ford	Nissan	BMW
Frequency	5	8	6	3

3 The line graph shows the number of students late for school one week.
  a How many students were late on Tuesday?
  b On which day were 5 students late?
  c Describe the trend for the week.

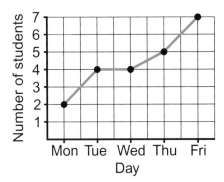

4 The graph shows the amount of water in a barrel over a 5-month period.
  a How much water was in the barrel in March?
  b In which months were there 50 gallons of water in the barrel?

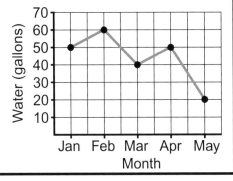

Pie charts

1   The pie chart shows the favourite
    type of chocolate of 32 women.
    a   How many of the women
        prefer plain chocolate?
    b   How many of the women
        prefer white chocolate?

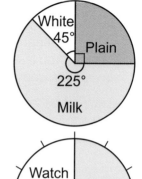

2   The pie chart shows the results
    of a survey of how 24 students
    spend their Saturday mornings.
    a   How many students watch TV?
    b   How many students shop?
    c   How many students work?

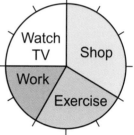

3   The table below shows the colours of 24 pairs of jeans:

Colour	Stonewash	Black	Untreated	Glitter
Frequency	3	7	10	4
Angle				

a   By copying and completing the table above, draw a pie
    chart to show the colours of the jeans.
b   What fraction of the jeans are untreated?
    Give your answer as a fraction in its lowest terms.

4   Here is the nutritional information for a 120 g jar of gravy
    granules:

Nutritional information	120 g
Protein	12 g
Carbohydrate	60 g
Fat	40 g
Sodium	8 g

Draw a pie chart to show the nutritional information.

Speedy Revision

Stem & leaf diagrams; scatter graphs

1 Here are the heights of 23 people in centimetres.

131, 136, 138, 143, 146, 148, 153, 154, 155, 158, 159, 160, 162, 164, 165, 167, 168, 170, 171, 173, 178, 184, 187

Copy and complete the stem and leaf diagram for the data:

130	1
140	
150	
160	0 2
170	
180	

Key:

130	1

represents 131 cm

2 Here are the weights of 23 people in kilograms.

61, 67, 84, 93, 72, 57, 65, 86, 49, 63, 75, 69, 76, 69, 46, 70, 56, 71, 53, 48, 52, 54, 64

a Draw a stem and leaf diagram for the data.
Use multiples of 10 as the stems and units as the leaves.

b Use your diagram to find the median weight.

3 Nisha has collected some data that shows that the hotter the weather the more ice-creams are sold.
Which of these scatter graphs represents her data?

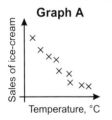
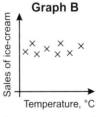
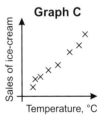

4 The table shows how far some people live from a cinema, and how often they went to the cinema last year.

Distance (km)	17	3	11	1	7	14	9	6
Number of visits	0	26	14	35	16	2	12	24

a Show the data as a scatter diagram.

b Describe the correlation for the data.

Mean, median, mode, range

1 Cycling routes are graded A, B or C.
Here are the grades of 15 routes:

B, C, A, B, C, B, B, C, A, C, B, A, A, C, C

What is the modal grade?

2 Find the mode for each of these sets of data:
   a Days in first 6 months: 31, 28, 31, 30, 31, 30
   b Hours spent driving: 4, 3, 4, 2, 3, 4, 2, 1, 2, 3, 3, 2, 2

3 Arrange each of these sets of data in order and find the median:
   a Number of pens: 7, 8, 4, 6, 2, 5, 4
   b Hours of sunshine: 4, 7, 2, 5, 7, 4, 1, 6

4 Find the mean for each of these sets of data:
   a Number of cars in a car park: 12, 32, 18, 15, 34
   b Pocket money: £5, £4, £2.50, £3, £9.50, £3, £15

5 Find the range for each of these sets of data:
   a Dress sizes: 8, 14, 12, 10, 18, 8, 8, 10, 12, 12, 16
   b Number of ants: 124, 200, 25, 32, 255
   c Mass of parcels in kilograms: 10, 4.5, 14.5, 5, 13.5, 7

6 Find the mean, median, mode and range for each of these sets of data:
   a Water in a cup in millilitres: 12, 12, 12, 14, 17, 20
   b Carrots in a bag: 23, 31, 15, 12, 23, 5, 17
   c Length of copper pipe in metres: 3, 4, 4, 6, 2, 3, 2.5

7 The frequency table shows the number of cars per household in Carrie's street.

Number of cars	0	1	2	3
Frequency	3	6	4	2

Find the mean number of cars per household.

8 Jerome received a mean of 2.4 text messages per day last month, with a range of 5 – 0 = 5. Kay received a mean of 1.9 per day last month, with a range of 3 – 1 = 2.
Which of them is more likely to get a text message today?

Speedy Revision

Probability

1 Copy this probability line:

Impossible ———+———————+———————+——— Certain

Show these events on your line:
a The next baby born is a girl.
b A horse passing a driving test.
c You will drink something tomorrow.
d Picking a Spade from a pack of ordinary playing cards.

2 Use a word from the box to describe each of these events:
a A man will swim the English channel tomorrow in 15 minutes.
b Rolling a 6 on a fair dice.
c Tossing a coin and getting tails.

> unlikely
> evens
> likely
> impossible

3 A fair dice is thrown.
a Find the probability of getting a 3.
b Find the probability of getting an odd number.

4 A letter is picked at random from the word PRINTER.
a What is the probability that the letter is T?
b What is the probability that the letter is R?

5 A bag contains 3 red marbles and 7 blue marbles.
A marble is drawn at random from the bag.
a Find the probability that the marble is red.
b What is the probability that the marble is green?

6 A 3-sided spinner is spun 100 times, with these results:

Colour	Purple	Red	Blue
Frequency	60	25	15

The spinner is spun one more time.
Estimate the probability of the spinner landing on:
a red   **b** purple.

7 The probability of winning a prize is 0.15.
What is the probability of not winning a prize?

8 A box contains black counters and white counters.
A counter is picked at random, replaced, then another counter is picked. List the possible outcomes.

Speedy Revision

53

Answers

Page 4 Special numbers

1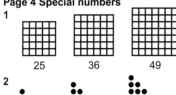

25   36   49

2

15   21   28

3   2, 3, 5, 7, 11, 13, 17, 19, 23, 29
4   **a** 43, 17, 23   **b** 25, 64, 36   **c** 10, 36

Page 4 Squares & square roots

1   **a** 25   **b** 49   **c** 100   **d** 16   **e** 64   **f** 81   **g** 36
   h 4900   **i** 400
2   **a** 9   **b** 225   **c** 169   **d** 144   **e** 2500
   f 196   **g** 10 000   **h** 324   **i** 441
3   **a** 4   **b** 7   **c** 5   **d** 11   **e** 2   **f** 8
4   **a** 10   **b** 15   **c** 14   **d** 20   **e** 25   **f** 18   **g** 34
   h 41   **i** 0.3

Page 5 Mental strategies for + and –

1   **a** 84   **b** 230   **c** 750   **d** 161   **e** 250   **f** 1001
   g 624   **h** 785   **i** 476
2   **a** 20   **b** 30   **c** 22   **d** 30   **e** 45   **f** 120
3   **a** 71   **b** 143   **c** 487   **d** 993   **e** 387   **f** 791
   g 699   **h** 210   **i** 816
4   **a** 143   **b** 542   **c** 251   **d** 265   **e** 117   **f** 123
   g 195   **h** 61   **i** 37
5   **a** 97   **b** 257   **c** 387   **d** 603   **e** 979   **f** 181
   g 512   **h** 733   **i** 755
6   **a** 56   **b** 429   **c** 561   **d** 288   **e** 203   **f** 408
   g 134   **h** 348   **i** 136
7   **a** 867   **b** 734   **c** 945   **d** 438   **e** 509   **f** 13
   g 132   **h** 958   **i** 441
8   367 cm
9   £116

Page 6 Written methods for + and –

1   **a** 298   **b** 1159   **c** 980   **d** 744   **e** 809   **f** 1857
2   **a** 24   **b** 211   **c** 85   **d** 162   **e** 117   **f** 1325
3   **a** 2.78   **b** 39.9   **c** 7.97   **d** 5.79
   e 3.93   **f** 160.7
4   **a** 1.84   **b** 4.11   **c** 2.12   **d** 13.12
   e 11.42   **f** 12.05
5   **a** 10.52   **b** 9.15   **c** 9.17   **d** 5.27
   e 68.2   **f** 9.63
6   **a** 4.19   **b** 7.62   **c** 19.44   **d** 7.19
   e 230.92   **f** 556.32

7   **a** £39.88   **b** £11.46   **c** £39.82   **d** £41.31
8   £23.43
9   £106.42

Page 7 Mult' and div' by 10, 100, 1000, ...

1   **a** 540   **b** 9000   **c** 500   **d** 63   **e** 80   **f** 200
   g 32   **h** 45   **i** 50.6
2   **a** 4   **b** 9.6   **c** 20   **d** 31.9   **e** 2.48   **f** 0.71
   g 1.11   **h** 41.6   **i** 5.1
3   **a** 5400   **b** 770   **c** 24 000   **d** 21 000
   e 2000   **f** 600
4   **a** 40   **b** 0.4   **c** 11   **d** 0.3   **e** 80   **f** 0.19

Page 7 Mental strategies for × and ÷

1   **a** 92   **b** 64   **c** 112   **d** 124
2   **a** 75   **b** 429   **c** 640   **d** 210   **e** 153   **f** 207
   g 242   **h** 320
3   **a** 1500   **b** 700   **c** 400   **d** 800
4   **a** 285   **b** 475   **c** 315   **d** 228   **e** 525   **f** 273
   g 840   **h** 570
5   **a** 120   **b** 98   **c** 630   **d** 468   **e** 196   **f** 816
   g 165   **h** 306
6   **a** 8   **b** 5   **c** 12   **d** 7

Page 8 Written multiplication

1   **a** 423   **b** 416   **c** 1107   **d** 834   **e** 1435
   f 871   **g** 756   **h** 1536
2   **a** 273   **b** 378   **c** 442   **d** 714   **e** 672   **f** 2528
   g 2280   **h** 3856
3   **a** 16.2   **b** 23.8   **c** 23.6   **d** 16.2   **e** 3.72
   f 22.08   **g** 15.95   **h** 14.85
4   **a** 18.2   **b** 24.6   **c** 29.6   **d** 24.5   **e** 27.54
   f 10.32   **g** 16.17   **h** 24.72
5   £16.45

Page 8 Written division

1   **a** 42   **b** 19   **c** 27   **d** 17   **e** 49   **f** 26
   g 29   **h** 16
2   **a** 19 remainder 1   **b** 13 remainder 7
   c 18 remainder 2   **d** 23 remainder 2
   e 17 remainder 3   **f** 41 remainder 1
   g 20 remainder 4   **h** 31 remainder 1
3   **a** 1.8   **b** 2.5   **c** 13.1   **d** 11.6   **e** 20.5   **f** 21.9
   g 20.4   **h** 16.8
4   86 strawberries

Page 9 Multiples, factors & prime factors

1   **a** 2, 4, 6, 8, 10   **b** 4, 8, 12, 16, 20
   c 10, 20, 30, 40, 50   **d** 7, 14, 21, 28, 35
   e 6, 12, 18, 24, 30   **f** 11, 22, 33, 44, 55
   g 3, 6, 9, 12, 15   **h** 20, 40, 60, 80, 100
2   **a** True   **b** True   **c** False   **d** False
   e True   **f** False   **g** False   **h** True

Answers

Page 9 Multiples, factors & prime factors (cont)

3 **a** 1, 3, 9, 27 **b** 1, 2, 7, 14
  c 1, 2, 3, 4, 6, 9, 12, 18, 36
  d 1, 2, 4, 5, 10, 20
  e 1, 2, 4, 5, 10, 20, 25, 50, 100
  f 1, 3, 7, 9, 21, 63 **g** 1, 7, 49
  h 1, 2, 4, 11, 22, 44

4 **a** 1, 19; prime **b** 1, 5, 25; not prime
  c 1, 3, 7, 21; not prime **d** 1, 17; prime

5 **a** 3, 18, 12 **b** 32, 12

6 **a** $2 \times 2 \times 7 = 2^2 \times 7$ **b** $3 \times 5 \times 7$
  c $3 \times 5 \times 5 = 3 \times 5^2$ **d** $2 \times 3 \times 13$
  e $2 \times 2 \times 5 \times 5 = 2^2 \times 5^2$
  f 2×23 **g** $2 \times 2 \times 5 \times 7 = 2^2 \times 5 \times 7$
  h $2 \times 3 \times 3 \times 5 = 2 \times 3^2 \times 5$

Page 9 LCM & HCF

1 **a** 9 **b** 40 **c** 24 **d** 48 **e** 75 **f** 42
  g 200 **h** 150

2 **a** 6 **b** 5 **c** 12 **d** 7 **e** 16 **f** 1 **g** 14 **h** 15

Page 10 Ordering numbers

1 2535

2 **a** 15, 17, 27, 99, 152, 181
  b 16, 58, 182, 209, 1001
  c 4, 6, 15, 72, 399, 409
  d 12, 21, 102, 112, 121
  e 2, 4, 39, 42, 257, 3006
  f 79, 96, 102, 480, 482, 531

3 **a** 0.43 **b** 1.67 **c** 5.79 **d** 1.92 **e** 30.19
  f 0.54 **g** 0.3 **h** 1.8 **i** 21.3

4 Earl

Page 10 Rounding & estimating

1 **a** 30 **b** 70 **c** 1070 **d** 240 **e** 4020

2 **a** 500 **b** 800 **c** 0 **d** 1300 **e** 1000

3 **a** 2000 **b** 1000 **c** 7000 **d** 7000 **e** 31 000

4 **a** 1 **b** 11 **c** 3 **d** 12 **e** 17

5 **a** 6.2 **b** 0.6 **c** 1.4 **d** 2.7 **e** 5.5 **f** 3.8
  g 4.8 **h** 7.1 **i** 1.6 **j** 3.1

6 **a** 1.44 **b** 9.03 **c** 4.94 **d** 10.84 **e** 0.61
  f 2.99 **g** 12.10 **h** 1.72

7 **a** 795 **b** 632 **c** 798 **d** 2881 **e** 1470
  f 1028 **g** 60.03 **h** 23.8 **i** 9

Page 11 Negative numbers

1 **a** 5°C **b** −5°C **c** −15°C **d** −8°C

2
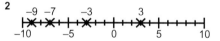

3 **a** −3, −1, 1, 2, 4
  b
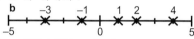

4 **a** −5°C **b** 7°C **c** −13°C

5 **a** −6 **b** −5 **c** 10 **d** 8 **e** −4 **f** −30
  g −21 **h** −110 **i** −9 **j** −2 **k** 3 **l** −3

Page 12 Fractions

1 **a** $\frac{1}{4}$ **b** $\frac{2}{4} = \frac{1}{2}$ **c** $\frac{3}{4}$ **d** $\frac{1}{5}$ **e** $\frac{2}{5}$
  f $\frac{3}{8}$ **g** $\frac{5}{9}$ **h** $\frac{5}{14}$

2 **a** Any one part shaded
  b Any three parts shaded
  c Any seven parts shaded

3 **a** $\frac{2}{8} = \frac{1}{4}$ **b** $\frac{3}{9} = \frac{1}{3}$ **c** $\frac{3}{12} = \frac{1}{4}$ **d** $\frac{2}{6} = \frac{1}{3}$
  e $\frac{6}{12} = \frac{3}{4} = \frac{1}{2}$ **f** $\frac{12}{48} = \frac{6}{24} = \frac{4}{16} = \frac{3}{12} = \frac{2}{8} = \frac{1}{4}$

4 **a** $\frac{1}{2}$ **b** $\frac{2}{3}$ **c** $\frac{2}{3}$ **d** $\frac{1}{2}$ **e** $\frac{2}{5}$
  f $\frac{1}{7}$ **g** ÷3 **h** ÷5 **i** ÷4, $\frac{2}{3}$

5 **a** $\frac{3}{4}$ **b** $\frac{1}{6}$ **c** $\frac{1}{3}$ **d** $\frac{1}{6}$ **e** $\frac{1}{3}$
  f $\frac{1}{4}$ **g** $\frac{3}{5}$ **h** $\frac{1}{10}$ **i** $\frac{1}{4}$

6 **a** $\frac{2}{5}$ **b** $\frac{3}{8}$ **c** $\frac{4}{9}$ **d** $\frac{3}{7}$ **e** $\frac{5}{6}$
  f $\frac{5}{8}$ **g** $\frac{6}{7}$ **h** $\frac{3}{8}$ **i** $\frac{5}{6}$

7 **a** $\frac{1}{3}$ **b** $\frac{1}{5}$ **c** $\frac{1}{7}$ **d** $\frac{2}{5}$ **e** $\frac{3}{8}$
  f $\frac{5}{8}$ **g** $\frac{2}{9}$ **h** $\frac{1}{9}$ **i** $\frac{1}{6}$

8 **a** $\frac{1}{2}$ **b** $\frac{1}{3}$ **c** $\frac{1}{2}$ **d** $\frac{3}{4}$ **e** $\frac{1}{4}$
  f $\frac{1}{5}$ **g** $\frac{3}{4}$ **h** $\frac{1}{2}$ **i** $\frac{1}{6}$

9 **a** $\frac{3}{2}$ **b** $\frac{4}{3}$ **c** $\frac{7}{4}$ **d** $\frac{7}{5}$ **e** $\frac{13}{6}$
  f $\frac{17}{7}$ **g** $\frac{21}{8}$ **h** $\frac{31}{10}$ **i** $\frac{29}{9}$

10 **a** $3\frac{2}{3}$ **b** $6\frac{1}{2}$ **c** $4\frac{1}{6}$ **d** $3\frac{2}{5}$ **e** $2\frac{2}{9}$
  f $5\frac{1}{4}$ **g** $2\frac{1}{2}$ **h** $2\frac{3}{8}$ **i** $3\frac{1}{7}$

11 **a** $\frac{1}{2}, \frac{2}{3}, \frac{9}{12}$ **b** $\frac{4}{9}, \frac{11}{18}, \frac{2}{3}$ **c** $\frac{3}{5}, \frac{13}{20}, \frac{3}{4}$

12 **a** $5\frac{1}{2}$ **b** $\frac{7}{4}$

13 **a** £30 **b** £30 × 2 = £60

14 **a** 25 m **b** 25 m × 3 = 75 m

15 **a** 7 mm **b** 7 mm × 2 = 14 mm

16 **a** 4p **b** 4p × 7 = 28p

17 240°

18 30 g

19 **a** $\frac{1}{6}$ **b** $\frac{2}{15}$ **c** $\frac{2}{7}$

20 **a** $\frac{2}{3}$ **b** $\frac{7}{10}$ **c** $\frac{4}{15}$

Answers

Page 15 Percentages
1 40% 2 25% 3 30%
4 a £1.50 b 36 g
5 a 13.6 cm b 54p
6 a 200 ml b £12 c 6 g d 18 mm e £94.50
 f 17.7 m
7 a 33p b 18 mm c 126 g d 100 m
 e £62.40 f 58.5 litres
8 a 63p b 57 mm c £19.20 d 119 g
 e £18 400 f 34 litres
9 £9.60 10 105 mm 11 £241.50

Page 16 Fractions, decimals & percentages
1 a 0.01 b 0.125 c 0.6 d 0.875 e 0.15
 f 0.54 g 0.333... h 0.3
2 a $\frac{17}{100}$ b $\frac{23}{100}$ c $\frac{3}{100}$ d $\frac{29}{100}$
 e $\frac{30}{100} = \frac{3}{10}$ f $\frac{75}{100} = \frac{3}{4}$
 g $\frac{15}{100} = \frac{3}{20}$ h $\frac{12}{100} = \frac{3}{25}$
3 a 5% b 62% c 18% d 94% e 30%
 f 10% g $33\frac{1}{3}$% h 80%
4 a 0.4 b 0.25 c 0.9 d 0.6 e 0.5 f 0.18
 g 0.32 h 0.99
5 a $\frac{5}{10} = \frac{1}{2}$ b $\frac{1}{10}$ c $\frac{75}{100} = \frac{3}{4}$ d $\frac{7}{10}$
 e $\frac{6}{10} = \frac{3}{5}$ f $\frac{13}{100}$ g $\frac{49}{100}$ h $\frac{45}{100} = \frac{9}{20}$
6 $\frac{2}{5}$ of £40 (= £16, 25% of £60 = £15)

Page 16 Ratio & proportion
1 a $\frac{1}{3}$ b $\frac{1}{4}$ c $\frac{2}{5}$ d $\frac{2}{6} = \frac{1}{3}$ e $\frac{6}{10} = \frac{3}{5}$
2 a $\frac{2}{3}$ b $\frac{3}{4}$ c $\frac{3}{5}$ d $\frac{4}{6} = \frac{2}{3}$ e $\frac{4}{10} = \frac{2}{5}$
3 a 1 : 2 b 1 : 3 c 2 : 3 d 2 : 4 = 1 : 2
 e 6 : 4 = 3 : 2
4 16 : 14 = 8 : 7
5 12 : 8 = 3 : 2
6 105p = £1.05
7 £6
8 175p ÷ 7 = 25p each, 25p × 3 = 75p
9 160p ÷ 5 = 32p each, 32p × 9 = £2.88
10 160 g ÷ 4 = 40 g, 40 g × 7 = 280 g

Page 17 Calculations with brackets
1 a 13 b 20 c 3 d 16 e 40 f 32 g 22
 h 22 i 4 j 11
2 a Not needed b 15 − (3 + 2) = 10
 c 8 × (4 + 6) = 80 d (3 + 8) × 12 = 132
 e 36 ÷ (6 + 3) = 4 f Not needed
 g 7 × (8 − 3) ÷ 5 = 7 h Not needed
 i (8 + 7 − 3) × 4 = 48 j Not needed

Page 18 Using letters
1 $b + 1$
2 $c + 3$
3 $s - 1$
4 $m - 2$
5 $10 \times c = 10c$
6 $5 \times b = 5b$
7 a $2g$ b $5c$ c $3t$ d nm e yz f ab g $10rs$
 h $4pq$ i $7cd$
8 a $3y$ b $4z$ c $4a$ d $7p$ e $2d$ f $6s$ g $3n$
 h $16r$ i $15b$ j $10t$
9 a $2w + 6$ b $3y + 3$ c $8s + 6$ d $5a + 6$
 e $4n + 2$ f $7m + 2$ g $7b + 2$ h $7c + 3$
 i $8t + 7$ j $4g + 8$

Page 19 Brackets & algebraic fractions
1 a $2x + 2$ b $5y - 15$ c $3n + 6$ d $8a - 8b$
 e $-4c - 4$ f $6x + 30$ g $-3z - 12$
 h $10w - 10$ i $-2t + 2$
2 a $3a + 5$ b $3n - 6$ c $12 - 5p$ d $8 - 2z$
3 a $\frac{2x}{5}$ b $\frac{2x}{3}$ c $\frac{3x}{8}$ d $\frac{3z}{7}$ e $\frac{7d}{10}$
 f $\frac{9n}{2}$ g $\frac{7a}{3}$ h $\frac{5a}{4}$ i $\frac{m}{9}$

Page 19 Equations
1 a $x = 2$ b $x = 10$ c $p = 3$ d $m = 4$
 e $p = 33$ f $x = 9$ g $y = 9$ h $c = 7$
 i $y = 4$ j $a = 16$
2 a $x = 2$ b $x = 4$ c $x = 4$ d $x = 5$ e $x = 10$
 f $x = 2$ g $x = 9$ h $x = 5$ i $x = 8$ j $x = 3$
3 a $x = 3$ b $x = 7$ c $x = 11$ d $x = 2$ e $x = 4$
 f $x = 5$ g $x = 4$ h $x = 5$ i $x = 2$ j $x = 6$
4 a $x = 2$ b $x = 9$ c $x = 4$ d $x = 3$ e $x = 11$
 f $x = 5$ g $x = 0$ h $x = 1$ i $x = 4$ j $x = 2$
5 a $6x$ centimetres b $x = 7$

Page 20 Formulae & substitution
1 a 11 b 3 c 14 d 24 e 80 f 56 g 20
 h 19 i 49
2 a 50 mm b 130 mm c 70 mm d 80 mm
 e 250 mm f 110 mm
3 a 200 cm b 500 cm c 150 cm
 d 1000 cm e 80 cm f 240 cm
4 a $C = 22h$ b £110 c £154
5 a 60 mph b $S = \frac{D}{T}$ c $S = 25$ mph
 d 8.9 m/s
6 a 4 b 18 c 27 d 50 e 23 f 48
7 125 cm^3

Answers

Page 21 Sequences & number patterns
1   **a** 1, 3, 5, 7, 9 **b** 5, 8, 11, 14, 17
    c 8, 9, 10, 11, 12 **d** 20, 18, 16, 14, 12
    e 2, 4, 8, 16, 32 **f** 30, 25, 20, 15, 10
    g 144, 72, 36, 18, 9 **h** 4, 12, 36, 108, 324
2   **a** Start at 2 and add 2
    b Start at 5 and add 5
    c Start at 100 and subtract 1
    d Start at 4 and add 6
    e Start at 36 and subtract 6
    f Start at 1 and multiply by 3
    g Start at 800 and halve
    h Start at 5 and double
3   **a** 15, 18, 21 **b** 50, 60, 70
    c 32, 64, 128 **d** 70, 65, 60
    e 27, 32, 37 **f** 12, 10, 8
    g 20, 10, 5 **h** 26, 29, 32
4   **a**

   b Start with 2 squares and add 2 squares
   c 16 squares, 20 squares **d** $2n$
5   **a**

   b Start with 4 matches and add 3 matches
   c 25 matches, 31 matches **d** $1 + 3n$
6   **a** 6, 7, 8, 9, 10 **b** 6, 12, 18, 24, 30
    c 0, 1, 2, 3, 4 **d** 10, 20, 30, 40, 50
    e 3, 5, 7, 9, 11 **f** 4, 9, 14, 19, 24
    g 7, 10, 13, 16, 19 **h** 19, 18, 17, 16, 15
    i 3, 8, 13, 18, 23
7   **a** 98 **b** 70 **c** 40
8   **a** $2n$ **b** $5n$ **c** $n + 7$ **d** $n + 100$
    e $2n + 1$ **f** $2n - 1$

Page 23 Functions & mappings
1   **a** $-1, 1, 6, x - 4$ **b** 4
2   ×5
3   **a** 5, 8, 11, $3x + 2$ **b** 5
4   $1 \rightarrow 10$
    $2 \rightarrow 15$
    $3 \rightarrow 20$
5   $x \rightarrow 5(x + 1)$
6   **a** $1 \rightarrow 4$
       $2 \rightarrow 8$
       $3 \rightarrow 12$
    b $1 \rightarrow -3$
       $2 \rightarrow -1$
       $3 \rightarrow 1$
    c $1 \rightarrow 6$
       $2 \rightarrow 9$
       $3 \rightarrow 12$

Page 24 Coordinates
1   **a** A(−2, 2), D(−3, −2)
    b

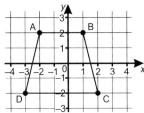

   c Isosceles trapezium
2   A(2, 4), B(5, 0), C(6, 8), D(0, 1),
    E(−8, 0), F(−4, 2), G(0, −3), H(−6, −2),
    I(2, −8), J(−4, −6)

Page 25 Straight-line graphs
1   **a**

x	−3	−2	−1	0	1
$y = x + 2$	−1	0	1	2	3

   b

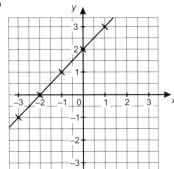

2   **a** 3 **b** −1 **c** 2
3   **a** Diagonal **b** Horizontal **c** Diagonal
    d Vertical **e** Diagonal **f** Diagonal
    g Horizontal **h** Diagonal **i** Vertical
4   **a**

x	−3	−2	−1	0	1	2
$y = 2x + 3$	−3	−1	1	3	5	7

Answers

Page 25 Straight-line graphs (cont)

b

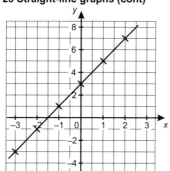

5 **a** $y = 4$ **b** $x = 4$ **c** $y = -x$ **d** $y = x$

Page 27 Real-life graphs

1 **a**

Amount in £	0	10	20	30	40	50
Amount in €	0	14	28	42	56	70

b

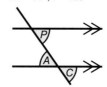

2 **A** Jenny leaves home at 09:00 and cycles to the shop. The shop is 3 miles away, and it takes her 10 minutes.
B Jenny stays at the shop for 10 minutes.
C Jenny is cycling home.
D After 10 minutes she meets her sister, Susie. She walks the remaining 0.4 miles with Susie. Jenny arrives home at 09:40.

Page 28 Units of measurement

1 **a** 100 cm **b** 10 mm **c** 1000 m
d 1000 g **e** 1000 ml
2 **a** 12 inches **b** 3 feet
c 16 ounces **d** 8 pints
3 **a** 30 cm **b** 1.6 km **c** 450 g **d** 30 g
e 2 pints

4 **a** 300 cm **b** 400 cm **c** 1000 cm
d 2300 cm **e** 5000 cm **f** 50 cm
5 **a** 20 mm **b** 50 mm **c** 110 mm
d 360 mm **e** 750 mm **f** 15 mm
6 **a** 3000 m **b** 4000 m **c** 10 000 m
d 23 000 m **e** 50 000 m **f** 2500 m
7 **a** 2000 g **b** 5000 g **c** 15 000 g
d 3000 ml **e** 9000 ml **f** 18 000 ml
8 **a** 20 cm **b** 3 km **c** 8 m **d** 5 litres
e 7 kg **f** 14 litres
9 **a** 4.5 cm **b** 0.5 kg **c** 6.5 litres **d** 62 mm
e 150 cm **f** 500 m

Page 29 Appropriate units & reading scales

1 **a** centimetres **b** metres **c** millilitres
d kilograms **e** litres **f** grams
g millimetres **h** kilometres
2 **a** 30 mm or 3 cm **b** 45 mm or 4.5 cm
c 97 mm or 9.7 cm
3 **a** 35 **b** 28 **c** 70 **d** 140 **e** 37 km/h **f** 7.8°C

Page 30 Estimating & measuring angles

1 **a** 90° **b** 180° **c** 270° **d** 360°
2 **a i** Between 100° and 110° **ii** 105°
b i Between 25° and 35° **ii** 30°
c i Between 130° and 140° **ii** 135°
d i Between 320° and 340° **ii** 327°

Page 30 Angles & parallel lines

1 **a** Obtuse angle **b** Acute angle
c Right angle **d** Reflex angle
2 **a** 180° **b** 360°
c Vertically opposite angles
3 **a** 145° **b** 26° **c** 115° **d** 92° **e** 60°
f $h = 55°$, $i = 125°$
4

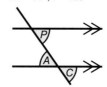

5 **a** 124° **b** 118° **c** $x = 78°$, $w = 78°$
d $y = 76°$, $z = 82°$

Page 32 Polygons

1 **a** 180° **b** 360°
2 **a** 40° **b** 27° **c** $x = 95°$, $y = 148°$ **d** $z = 60°$
3 **a** 90° **b** 92° **c** 92° **d** 210°
4 **a** 360° **b** (number of sides − 2) × 180°
5 **a** 6 **b** 120° **c** 60°

Speedy Revision

Answers

Page 33 Symmetry & properties of shapes

1 a   b

   c   d

2   a i 3   ii 3   b i 0   ii 2
   c i 2   ii 2   d i 4   ii 4

3   a A, E, H, M, T, U, W   b H, N, S, Z   c F, P

4   a 4   b 4

5   a Equilateral triangle   b Trapezium
   c Isosceles triangle   d Kite
   e Right-angled triangle   f Parallelogram

6

Name of polygon	Number of sides	All sides equal?	All angles equal?	Number of lines of symmetry	Order of rotation symmetry
Square	4	Yes	Yes	4	4
Rectangle	4	No	Yes	2	2
Isosceles triangle	3	No	No	1	1
Equilateral triangle	3	Yes	Yes	3	3
Rhombus	4	Yes	No	2	2
Kite	4	No	No	1	1
Trapezium	4	No	No	0	1
Regular pentagon	5	Yes	Yes	5	5
Parallelogram	4	No	No	0	2

Page 35 Reflection

1 a   b

   c   d

2   a   b

2   a 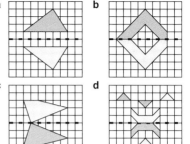   b

   c 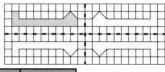   d

3

Page 36 Rotation

1   a

   b

   c

   d

2   a   b

Answers

Page 36 Rotation (cont)

c   d

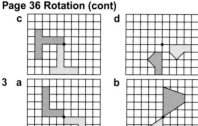

3   a   b

Page 37 Translation

1   a   b

2   a   b

3   a   b

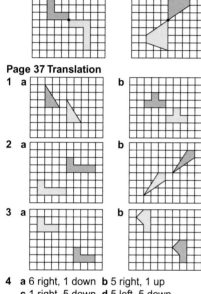

4   **a** 6 right, 1 down   **b** 5 right, 1 up
   c 1 right, 5 down   **d** 5 left, 5 down
   e 8 left, 4 up   **f** 4 right, 1 up
   g 1 left, 5 down   **h** 12 right, 1 up

Page 38 Enlargement

1   a   b

c

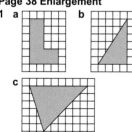

2   a   b

c

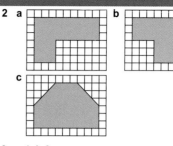

3   **a** 4   **b** 3

4

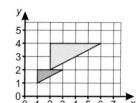

5   **a** 4   **b** (0, 1)

Page 39 Perimeter & circumference

1   **a** 10 cm   **b** 14 cm   **c** 14 cm   **d** 14 cm
2   **a** 32 cm   **b** 40 cm
3   **a** 18.8 cm   **b** 28.3 cm   **c** 25.1 cm
4   **a** 12.9 cm   **b** 18.3 cm

Page 40 Area of 2-D shapes

1   **a** 10 cm^2 **b** 5 cm^2 **c** 18 cm^2 **d** 10.5 m^2
2   **a** 48 cm^2 **b** 76 cm^2
3   **a** 8 cm^2 **b** 15 cm^2
4   **a** 10 cm^2 **b** 18 cm^2
5   **a** 6 m^2 **b** 17 m^2
6   **a** 78.5 cm^2 **b** 153.9 cm^2 **c** 95.0 cm^2

Page 41 Nets & 3-D shapes; plans & elevations

1   **a** and **c**
2   **a** Triangular prism
   b Regular tetrahedron
   c Square-based pyramid

Answers

Page 41 Nets & 3-D shapes; plans & elevations (cont)

3 a b

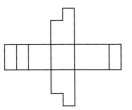

c

4 a

Plan   Front   Side

b

Plan   Front   Side

c

Plan   Front   Side

d
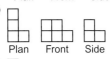

Plan   Front   Side

5 a
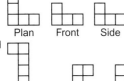

b

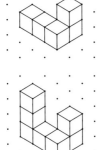

Page 42 Surface area

1 a 6 cm^2 b 10 cm^2 c 14 cm^2
  d 22 cm^2 e 24 cm^2 f 14 cm^2
2 a 16 cm^2 b 22 cm^2 c 54 cm^2 d 52 cm^2
3 4 m

Page 43 Volume

1 a 6 cm^3 b 8 cm^3 c 8 cm^3
2 a 4 cm^3 b 5 cm^3 c 144 cm^3 d 27 m^3
3 a i 4 cm^2 ii 28 cm^3 b i 21 m^2 ii 210 m^3
4 216 m^3

Page 44 Bearings & scale drawings

1 a 050° b 305°
2 a 150 km b 250 km c 1000 km
3 a 2 cm b 10 cm c 0.5 cm
4 a 130° b 040° c 220° d 8 km
  e 17 km f 15 km

Page 45 Constructions & loci

5

5 cm

6
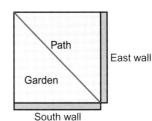

Path

East wall

Garden

South wall

7
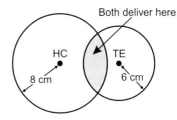

Both deliver here

HC   TE

8 cm   6 cm

Answers

Page 47 Collecting data & two-way tables

1   a Question 1: The options are too vague: 'occasionally' could mean different things to different people. Jenny should give definite options such as 'less than once a month', 'at least once a month but not every week', 'every week'.
    Question 2: Leading question: never start a question 'Do you agree...'
    Question 3: Too personal and not really relevant.
  b At that time, people who go to work or school will not be surveyed.
    People outside the swimming pool are likely to like the swimming pool, so Jenny will miss people who do not like it.

2   Primary data is data you collect yourself. Secondary data is data that other people have collected.

3

	MP3	MP4	Total
Boys own	15	6	21
Girls own	17	3	20
Total	32	9	41

4

	Red	Blue	Silver	Total
Trek	3	4	2	9
Giant	5	6	4	15
Total	8	10	6	24

Total number of bikes = 24

Page 48 Frequency tables

1

Colour of book	Tally	Frequency
Yellow	卌	5
Orange	卌	5
Purple	卌 卌	10
	Total	20

2

No. of people	Tally	Frequency
1	IIII	4
2	卌	5
3	III	3
4	II	2
5	I	1
	Total	15

3   a

No. of potatoes	Tally	Frequency
26 to 35	卌 II	7
36 to 45	卌 III	8
46 to 55	卌	5
	Total	20

b

No. of potatoes	Tally	Frequency
$20 \leqslant N < 30$	III	3
$30 \leqslant N < 40$	卌 II	7
$40 \leqslant N < 50$	卌 II	7
$50 \leqslant N < 60$	III	3
	Total	20

Page 49 Bar charts & line graphs

1   5 + 4 + 7 = 16 medals

2

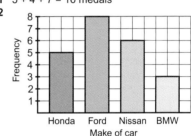

3   a 4 students   b Thursday
    c The number of late students increases as the week goes along.

4   a 40 gallons   b January and April

Page 50 Pie charts

1   a 8 women   b 4 women

2   a 6 students   b 8 students   c 4 students

3   a Angles: 45°, 105°, 150°, 60°

b $\frac{10}{24} = \frac{5}{12}$

Speedy Revision

Answers

Page 50 Pie charts (cont)

4 Angles: Protein 36°, Carbohydrate 180°, Fat 120°, Sodium 24°

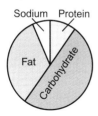

Page 51 Stem & leaf diagrams; scatter graphs

1

130	1 6 8
140	3 6 8
150	3 4 5 8 9
160	0 2 4 5 7 8
170	0 1 3 8
180	4 7

Key:

130	1

represents 131 cm

2 a

40	6 8 9
50	2 3 4 6 7
60	1 3 4 5 7 9 9
70	0 1 2 5 6
80	4 6
90	3

Key:

40	6

represents 46 kg

  b 65 kg

3 Graph C

4 a

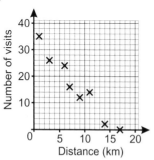

  b Strong negative correlation (people who live further from the cinema go less often)

Page 52 Mean, median, mode, range

1 C

2 a 31 days b 2 hours

3 a 2, 4, 4, 5, 6, 7, 8; median = 5 pens
   b 1, 2, 4, 4, 5, 6, 7, 7; median = 4.5 hours

4 a 22.2 cars b £6

5 a 10 b 230 ants c 10 kg

6 a Mean = 14.5 ml, median = 13 ml
     mode = 12 ml, range = 8 ml
   b Mean = 18 carrots, median = 17 carrots
     mode = 23 carrots, range = 26 carrots
   c Mean = 3.5 m, median = 3 m
     mode = 3 m and 4 m, range = 4 m

7 $1\frac{1}{3}$ cars

8 Although Jerome gets more text messages on average, the range shows that some days he gets none at all. Kay's range shows that she had at least one text message every day last month, so she is more likely to get one today.

Page 53 Probability

1

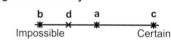

2 a Impossible b Unlikely c Evens

3 a $\frac{1}{6}$ b $\frac{3}{6} = \frac{1}{2}$

4 a $\frac{1}{7}$ b $\frac{2}{7}$

5 a $\frac{3}{10}$ b 0

6 a $\frac{25}{100} = \frac{1}{4}$ b $\frac{60}{100} = \frac{3}{5}$

7 $1 - 0.15 = 0.85$

8 Black then black, black then white, white then black, white then white

Speedy Revision